John Nicholson

The preceptor

Being a simple system for enabling young men to acquire a knowledge of

the doctrines of the gospel

John Nicholson

The preceptor
*Being a simple system for enabling young men to acquire a knowledge of the
doctrines of the gospel*

ISBN/EAN: 9783337257248

Printed in Europe, USA, Canada, Australia, Japan

Cover: Foto ©Thomas Meinert / pixelio.de

More available books at **www.hansebooks.com**

THE

PRECEPTOR.

BEING A

*SIMPLE SYSTEM FOR ENABLING YOUNG
MEN TO ACQUIRE A KNOWLEDGE
OF THE DOCTRINES OF THE
GOSPEL, AND THE ABILITY
TO PREACH THEM.*

By Elder John Nicholson.

Entered according to Act of Congress, in the year 1883, by John Nicholson, in
the office of the Librarian of Congress, at Washington.

SALT LAKE CITY:
DESERET NEWS COMPANY, PRINTERS AND PUBLISHERS.

1883.

PREFACE.

I have long thought that there should be some simple method of teaching the young men of the Church the doctrines of the Gospel of Christ, and at the same time enabling them to acquire the ability to preach them.

This need receives many illustrations in the awkward predicament in which many young and inexperienced Elders are placed when first entering the missionary field with little or no previous training.

This subject was directly forced upon my attention in the early part of January, 1883, when a committee, representing eleven young men, waited upon me, with a request that I should instruct them in acquiring an understanding of what are termed the first principles of the Gospel.

I undertook this labor, and was amply rewarded by the marked progress made by the class in a comparatively brief time.

The gratifying results have led me to publish a synopsis of the system, in the hope that other brethren may make a practical application of it and thus more extended good be produced.

INDEX.

THE PRECEPTOR.

CHAPTER I.

PREPARATION FOR CLASS EXERCISES.

By way of preparation, before the opening of organized exercises, each pupil should be required to carefully read many times over, and reflect upon the doctrines and principles contained in them, the following passages of scripture, which are given in full. Other passages bearing on the same subjects should also be sought out and studied:

SCRIPTURE PASSAGES. — FIRST PRINCIPLES OF THE GOSPEL.

Faith and Works.

Showing works as well as faith are required to insure salvation—

James, second chapter:

14 What doth it profit, my brethren, though a man say he hath faith, and have not works? can faith save him?

15 If a brother or sister be naked, and destitute of daily food,

16 And one of you say unto them, Depart in peace, be ye warmed and filled; notwithstanding ye give them not those things which are needful to the body; what doth it profit?

17 Even so faith, if it hath not works, is dead, being alone.

18 Yea, a man may say, Thou hast faith, and I have works: shew me thy faith without thy works, and I will shew thee my faith by my works.

19 Thou believest that there is one God; thou doest well: the devils also believe, and tremble.

20 But wilt thou know, O vain man, that faith without works is dead?

21 Was not Abraham our father justified by works, when he had offered Isaac his son upon the altar?

22 Seest thou how faith wrought with his works, and by works was faith made perfect?

23 And the Scripture was fulfilled which saith, Abraham believed God, and it was imputed unto him for righteousness: and he was called the Friend of God.

24 Ye see then how that by works a man is justified, and not by faith only.

25 Likewise also was not Rahab the harlot justified by works, when she had received the messengers, and had sent them out another way?

26 For as the body without the spirit is dead, so faith without works is dead also.

Hebrews, eleventh chapter:

3 Through faith we understand that the worlds were framed by the word of God, so that things which are seen were not made of things which do appear.

32 And what shall I more say? for the time would fail me to tell of Gideon, and of Barak, and of Samson, and of Jephthah; of David also, and Samuel, and of the prophets:

33 Who through faith subdued kingdoms, wrought righteousness, obtained promises, stopped the mouths of lions,

34 Quenched the violence of fire, escaped the edge of the sword, out of weakness were made strong, waxed valiant in fight, turned to flight the armies of the aliens.

1 John, second chapter:

1 My little children, these things write I unto you, that ye sin not. And if any man sin, we have an advocate with the Father, Jesus Christ the righteous:

2 And he is the propitiation for our sins: and not for ours only, but also for the sins of the whole world.

3 And hereby we do know that we know him, if we keep his commandments.

4 He that saith, I know him, and keepeth not his commandments, is a liar, and the truth is not in him.

Acts, ninth chapter:

1 And Saul, yet breathing out threatenings and

slaughter against the disciples of the Lord, went unto the high priest,

2 And desired of him letters to Damascus to the synagogues, that if he found any of this way, whether they were men or women, he might bring them bound unto Jerusalem.

3 And as he journeyed, he came near Damascus: and suddenly there shined round about him a light from heaven:

4 And he fell to the earth, and heard a voice saying unto him, Saul, Saul, why persecutest thou me?

5 And he said, Who art thou, Lord? And the Lord said, I am Jesus whom thou persecutest: it is hard for thee to kick against the pricks.

6 And he trembling and astonished said, Lord, what wilt thou have me to do? And the Lord said unto him, Arise, and go into the city, and it shall be told thee what thou must do.

Matt., second chapter:

21 Not every one that saith unto me, Lord, Lord, shall enter into the kingdom of heaven; but he that *doeth* the will of my Father which is in heaven.

Showing that devils not only believe but know that Jesus is the Christ—

I Tim., fourth chapter:

1 Now the spirit speaketh expressly, that in the latter times some shall depart from the faith, giving heed to seducing spirits and doctrines of devils.

Luke, fourth chapter:

41 And devils also came out of many, crying out

and saying, Thou art Christ the Son of God. And he rebuking them suffered them not to speak: for they knew that he was Christ.

Repentance and Baptism.

Showing the absolute essentiality of the administration of the ordinance of baptism— .

Mark, sixteenth chapter:

15 And he said unto them, Go ye into all the world, and preach the gospel to every creature.

16 He that believeth and is baptized shall be saved; but he that believeth not shall be damned.

17 And these signs shall follow them that believe; In my name shall they cast out devils; they shall speak with new tongues;

18 They shall take up serpents; and if they drink any deadly thing, it shall not hurt them; they shall lay hands on the sick, and they shall recover.

19 So then, after the Lord had spoken unto them, he was received up into heaven, and sat on the right hand of God.

20 And they went forth, and preached everywhere, the Lord working with them, and confirming the word with signs following. Amen.

John, third chapter:

1 There was a man of the Pharisees, named Nicodemus, a ruler of the Jews.

2 The same came to Jesus by night, and said unto him, Rabbi, we know that thou art a teacher come from God: for no man can do these miracles that thou doest, except God be with him.

3 Jesus answered and said unto him, Verily, verily, I say unto thee, except a man be born again, he cannot see the kingdom of God.

4 Nicodemus saith unto him, How can a man be born when he is old? can he enter the second time into his mother's womb, and be born?

5 Jesus answered, Verily, verily, I say unto thee, Except a man be born of water and of the Spirit, he cannot enter into the kingdom of God.

22 After these things came Jesus and his disciples into the land of Judea; and there he tarried with them, and baptized.

23 And John also was baptizing in Enon near to Salim, because there was much water there: and they came, and were baptized.

Matt., third chapter:

13 Then cometh Jesus from Galilee to Jordan unto John, to be baptized of him.

14 But John forbade him, saying, I have need to be baptized of thee, and comest thou to me?

15 And Jesus answering said unto him, Suffer it to be so now: for thus it becometh us to fulfil all righteousness. Then he suffered him.

16 And Jesus, when he was baptized, went up straightway out of the water: and lo, the heavens were opened unto him, and he saw the Spirit of God descending like a dove, and lighting upon him.

17 And lo, a voice from heaven, saying, This is my beloved Son, in whom I am well pleased.

Luke, seventh chapter:

28 For I say unto you, Among those that are born of women there is not a greater prophet than John

the Baptist: but he that is least in the kingdom of God is greater than he.

29 And all the people that heard him, and the publicans, justified God, being baptized with the baptism of John.

30 But the Pharisees and lawyers rejected the counsel of God against themselves, being not baptized of him.

Showing immersion to be the proper mode of baptism—

Romans, sixth chapter:

3 Know ye not that so many of us as were baptized into Jesus Christ were baptized into his death?

4 Therefore we are buried with him by baptism into death: that like as Christ was raised up from the dead by the glory of the Father, even so we also should walk in newness of life.

5 For if we have been planted together in the likeness of his death, we shall be also in the likeness of his resurrection:

Col., second chapter:

11 In whom also ye are circumcised with the circumcision made without hands, in putting off the body of the sins of the flesh by the circumcision of Christ:

12 Buried with him in baptism, wherein also ye are risen with him through the faith of the operation of God, who hath raised him from the dead.

Eph., fourth chapter:

4 There is one body, and one Spirit, even as ye are called in one hope of your calling;

5 One Lord, one faith, *one* baptism,

6 One God and Father of all, who is above all, and through all, and in you all.

Showing that the object of baptism is the remission of sins and that repentance is a preparatory condition previous to its administration—

Acts, second chapter:

36 Therefore let all the house of Israel know assuredly, that God hath made that same Jesus, whom ye have crucified, both Lord and Christ.

37 Now when they heard this, they were pricked in their heart, and said unto Peter and to the rest of the apostles, Men and brethren, what shall we do?

38 Then Peter said unto them, Repent, and be baptized every one of you in the name of Jesus Christ for the remission of sins, and ye shall receive the gift of the Holy Ghost.

39 For the promise is unto you, and to your children, and to all that are afar off, even as many as the Lord our God shall call.

Acts, tenth chapter:

43 To him give all the prophets witness, that through his name whosoever believeth in him shall receive remission of sins.

44 While Peter yet spake these words, the Holy Ghost fell on all them which heard the word.

45 And they of the circumcision which believed were astonished, as many as came with Peter, because that on the Gentiles also was poured out the gift of the Holy Ghost.

46 For they heard them speak with tongues, and magnify God. Then answered Peter,

47 Can any man forbid water, that these should not be baptized, which have received the Holy Ghost as well as we?

48 And he commanded them to be baptized in the name of the Lord. Then prayed they him to tarry certain days.

Mark, first chapter:

4 John did baptize in the wilderness, and preach the baptism of repentance for the remission of sins.

5 And there went out unto him all the land of Judea, and they of Jerusalem, and were all baptized of him in the river of Jordan, confessing their sins.

Acts, twenty-second chapter:

6 And it came to pass, that, as I made my journey, and was come nigh unto Damascus about noon, suddenly there shone from heaven a great light round about me.

7 And I fell unto the ground, and heard a voice saying unto me, Saul, Saul, why persecutest thou me?

8 And I answered, Who art thou, Lord? And he said unto me, I am Jesus of Nazareth, whom thou persecutest.

9 And they that were with me saw indeed the light, and were afraid; but they heard not the voice of him that spake to me.

10 And I said, What shall I do, Lord? And the Lord said unto me, Arise, and go into Damascus; and there it shall be told thee of all things which are appointed for thee to do.

11 And when I could not see for the glory of that

light, being led by the hand of them that were with
me, I came into Damascus.

12 And one Ananias, a devout man according to
the law, having a good report of all the Jews which
dwelt there,

13 Came unto me, and stood, and said unto me,
Brother Saul, receive thy sight.   And the same hour
I looked up upon him.

14 And he said, The God of our fathers hath
chosen thee, that thou shouldest know his will, and
see that Just One, and shouldest hear the voice of
his mouth.

15 For thou shalt be his witness unto all men of
what thou hast seen and heard.

16 And now why tarriest thou? arise, and be baptized, and wash away thy sins, calling on the name
of the Lord.

The Holy Ghost.

The manner in which the Holy Ghost is
imparted—

Acts, eighth chapter:

12 But when they believed Philip preaching the
things concerning the kingdom of God, and the
name of Jesus Christ, they were baptized, both men
and women.

13 Then Simon himself believed also; and when
he was baptized, he continued with Philip, and wondered, beholding the miracles and signs which were
done.

14 Now when the apostles which were at Jerusalem heard that Samaria had received the word of
God, they sent unto them Peter and John:

15 Who, when they were come down, prayed for them, that they might receive the Holy Ghost:

16 (For as yet he was fallen upon none of them: only they were baptized in the name of the Lord Jesus.)

17 Then laid they their hands on them, and they received the Holy Ghost.

Acts, nineteenth chapter:

1 And it came to pass, that, while Apollos was at Corinth, Paul having passed through the upper coasts came to Ephesus; and finding certain disciples,

2 He said unto them, Have ye received the Holy Ghost since ye believed? And they said unto him, We have not so much as heard whether there be any Holy Ghost.

3 And he said unto them, Unto what then were ye baptized? And they said, Unto John's baptism.

4 Then said Paul, John verily baptized with the baptism of repentance, saying unto the people, that they should believe on him which should come after him, that is, on Christ Jesus.

5 When they heard this, they were baptized in the name of the Lord Jesus.

6 And when Paul had laid his hands upon them, the Holy Ghost came on them; and they spake with tongues and prophesied.

ORGANIZATION AND OFFICERS.

The nature of the organization, the character of the officers and their permanency—

2

Eph., fourth chapter:

8 Wherefore he saith, When he ascended up on high, he led captivity captive, and gave gifts unto men.

11 And he gave some, apostles; and some, prophets; and some, evangelists; and some, pastors and teachers;

12 For the perfecting of the saints, for the work of the ministry, for the edifying of the body of Christ:

13 Till we all come in the unity of the faith, and of the knowledge of the Son of God, unto a perfect man, unto the measure of the stature of the fulness of Christ:

14 That we henceforth be no more children, tossed to and fro, and carried about with every wind of doctrine, by the sleight of men, and cunning craftiness, whereby they lie in wait to deceive.

1 Cor., twelfth chapter:

14 For the body is not one member, but many.

15 If the foot shall say, Because I am not the hand, I am not of the body; is it therefore not of the body?

16 And if the ear shall say, Because I am not the eye, I am not of the body; is it therefore not of the body?

17 If the whole body were an eye, where were the hearing? If the whole were hearing, where were the smelling?

18 But now hath God set the members every one of them in the body, as it hath pleased him.

19 And if they were all one member, where were the body?

20 But now are they many members, yet but one body?

21 And the eye cannot say unto the hand, I have no need of thee: nor again the head to the feet, I have no need of you.

27 Now ye are the body of Christ, and members in particular.

28 And God hath set some in the church, first apostles, secondarily prophets, thirdly teachers, after that miracles, then gifts of healings, helps, governments, diversities of tongues.

29 Are all apostles? are all prophets? are all teachers? are all workers of miracles?

1 Cor., thirteenth chapter:

8 Charity never faileth: but whether there be prophecies, they shall fail; whether there be tongues, they shall cease; whether there be knowledge, it shall vanish away.

9 For we know in part, and we prophesy in part.

10 But when that which is perfect is come, then that which is in part shall be done away.

Luke, tenth chapter:

1 After these things the Lord appointed other seventy also, and sent them two and two before his face into every city and place, whither he himself would come.

2 Therefore said he unto them, The harvest truly is great, but the laborers are few: pray ye therefore the Lord of the harvest, that he would send forth laborers into his harvest.

3 Go your ways: behold I send you forth as lambs among wolves.

4 Carry neither purse, nor scrip, nor shoes: and salute no man by the way.

5 And into whatsoever house ye enter, first say, Peace be to this house.

6 And if the son of peace be there, your peace shall rest upon it: if not, it shall turn to you again.

THE GOSPEL TO THE DEAD.

Showing where the spirit of the thief went to, that the Gospel is preached to the departed spirits, and for what purpose—

Luke, twenty-third chapter:

39 And one of the malefactors which were hanged railed on him, saying, If thou be Christ, save thyself and us.

40 But the other answering rebuked him, saying, Dost not thou fear God, seeing thou art in the same condemnation?

41 And we indeed justly; for we receive the due reward of our deeds; but this man hath done nothing amiss.

42 And he said unto Jesus, Lord, remember me when thou comest into thy kingdom.

43 And Jesus said unto him, Verily I say unto thee, *To-day* shalt thou be with me in paradise.

1 Peter, third chapter:

18 For Christ also hath once suffered for sins, the just for the unjust, that he might bring us to God, being put to death in the flesh, but quickened by the spirit:

19 By which also he went and preached unto the spirits in prison;

20 Which sometime were disobedient, when once the longsuffering of God waited in the days of Noah, while the ark was a preparing, wherein few, that is, eight souls were saved by water.

1 Peter, fourth chapter:

6 For, for this cause was the gospel preached also to them that are dead, that they might be judged according to men in the flesh, but live according to God in the spirit.

John, twentieth chapter:

11 But Mary stood without at the sepulchre weeping: and as she wept, she stooped down, and looked into the sepulchre,

12 And seeth two angels in white sitting, the one at the head, and the other at the feet, where the body of Jesus had lain.

13 And they say unto her, Woman, why weepest thou? She saith unto them, Because they have taken away my Lord, and I know not where they have laid him.

14 And when she had thus said, she turned herself back, and saw Jesus standing, and knew not that it was Jesus.

15 Jesus saith unto her, Woman, why weepest thou? whom seekest thou? She, supposing him to be the gardener, saith unto him, Sir, If thou have borne him hence, tell me where thou hast laid him, and I will take him away.

16 Jesus saith unto her, Mary. She turned herself, and saith unto him, Rabboni: which is to say, Master.

17 Jesus said unto her, Touch me not; for I am

not yet ascended to my Father; but go to my brethren, and say unto them, I ascend unto my Father, and your Father; and to my God and to your God.

It may be well to state here, incidentally, that the third and fourth Protestant articles of religion assert that—

"Christ died for us and was buried, so also it is believed he went down into hell." And that "He rose again from death, took again his body of flesh and bones, wherewith he ascended into heaven."

The following is again inserted as a re-assertion of the essentiality of baptism, on account of what follows—

John, third chapter:
5 Jesus answered, Verily, verily, I say unto thee, Except a man be born of water and of the Spirit, he cannot enter into the kingdom of God.

Showing the administration of ordinances, by proxy or substitution, for the dead—

1 Cor., fifteenth chapter:
12 Now if Christ be preached that he rose from the dead, how say some among you that there is no resurrection of the dead?
13 But if there be no resurrection of the dead, then is Christ not risen:
22 For as in Adam all die, even so in Christ shall all be made alive.

23 But every man in his own order: Christ the first fruits; afterward they that are Christ's at his coming.   ,

29 Else what shall they do which are baptized for the dead, if the dead rise not at all; why are they then baptized for the dead?

Showing that sins are remitted or forgiven beyond this life—

Matt., twelfth chapter:

31 Wherefore I say unto you, All manner of sin and blasphemy shall be forgiven unto men; but the blasphemy against the Holy Ghost shall not be forgiven unto men.

32 And whosoever speaketh a word against the Son of Man, it shall be forgiven him; but whosoever speaketh against the Holy Ghost, it shall not be forgiven him, neither in this world, neither in the world to come.

THE APOSTASY.

Showing a universal apostasy from the true Gospel—

Isaiah, twenty-fourth chapter:

5 The earth also is defiled under the inhabitants thereof; because they have transgressed the laws, changed the ordinance, broken the everlasting covenant.

Rev., seventeenth chapter:

1 And there came one of the seven angels which had the seven vials, and talked with me, saying unto

me, Come hither; I will shew unto thee the judgment of the great whore that sitteth upon many
waters;

‑2 With whom the kings of the earth have com-
mitted fornication, and the inhabitants of the earth
have been made drunk with the wine of her fornication.

3 So he carried me away in the Spirit into the
wilderness: and I saw a woman sit upon a scarlet
colored beast, full of names of blasphemy, having
seven heads and ten horns.

4 And the woman was arrayed in purple and scarlet color, and decked with gold and precious stones
and pearls, having a golden cup in her hand, full of
abominations and filthiness of her fornication;

5 And upon her forehead was a name written,
MYSTERY, BABYLON THE GREAT, THE
MOTHER OF HARLOTS AND ABOMINATIONS
OF THE EARTH.

6 And I saw the woman drunken with the blood
of the saints, and with the blood of the marytrs of
Jesus; and when I saw her, I wondered with great
admiration.

2 Thess., second chapter:

1 Now we beseech you, brethren, by the coming
of our Lord Jesus Christ, and by our gathering together unto him.

2 That ye be not soon shaken in mind, or be
troubled, neither by spirit, nor by word, nor by let-
ter as from us, as that the day of Christ is at hand.

3 Let no man deceive you by any means: for that
day shall not come, except there be a falling away

first, and that man of sin be revealed, the son of perdition.

1 Timothy, fourth chapter:

1 Now the Spirit spreaketh expressly, that in the latter times some shall depart from the faith, giving heed to seducing spirits, and doctrines of devils;

2 Speaking lies in hypocrisy; having their conscience seared with a hot iron;

3 Forbidding to marry, and commanding to abstain from meats, which God hath created to be received with thanksgiving of them which believe and know the truth.

2 Timothy, third chapter:

1 This know also, that in the last days perilous times shall come.

2 For men shall be lovers of their own selves, covetous, boasters, proud, blasphemers, disobedient to parents, unthankful, unholy,

3 Without natural affection, trucebreakers, false accusers, incontinent, fierce, despisers of those that are good,

4 Traitors, heady, highminded, lovers of pleasures more than lovers of God;

5 Having a form of godliness, but denying the power thereof; from such turn away.

Acts, twentieth chapter:

28 Take heed therefore unto yourselves, and to all the flock, over the which the Holy Ghost hath made you overseers, to feed the Church of God, which he hath purchased with his own blood.

29 For I know this, that after my departing shall

grievous wolves enter in among you, not sparing the flock.

30 Also of your own selves shall men arise speaking perverse things, to draw away disciples after them.

Showing the necessity of divine authority by revelation—

Hebrews, fifth chapter:

1 For every high priest taken from among men is ordained for men in things pertaining to God, that he may offer both gifts and sacrifices for sins:

2 Who can have compassion on the ignorant, and on them that are out of the way; for that he himself also is compassed with infirmity.

3 And by reason hereof he ought, as for the people, so also for himself, to offer for sins.

4 And no man taketh this honor unto himself, but he that is called of God, as was Aaron.

Exodus, twenty-eighth chapter:

1 And take thou unto thee Aaron thy brother, and his sons with him, from among the children of Israel, that he may minister unto me in the priest's office, even Aaron, Nadab and Abihu, Eleazer and Ithamar, Aaron's sons.

Matt., twenty-eighth chapter:

18 And Jesus came and spake unto them, saying All power is given unto me in heaven and in earth.

19 Go ye therefore, and teach all nations, bap-

tizing them in the name of the Father, and of the Son, and of the Holy Ghost:

20 Teaching them to observe all things whatsoever I have commanded you: and, lo, I am with you alway, even unto the end of the world. Amen.

Matt., eighteenth chapter:

18 Verily I say unto you, Whatsoever ye shall bind on earth shall be bound in heaven; and whatsoever ye shall loose on earth shall be loosed in heaven.

2 Cor., fifth chapter:

20 Now then we are ambassadors for Christ, as though God did beseech you by us: we pray you in Christ's stead, be ye reconciled to God.

Titus, first chapter:

5 For this cause left I thee in Crete, that thou shouldest set in order the things that are wanting, and ordain elders in every city, as I had appointed thee.

RESTORATION OF THE GOSPEL.

The restoration of the Gospel in the latter days predicted—

Matt., twenty-fourth chapter:

3 And as he sat upon the mount of Olives, the disciples came unto him privately, saying, Tell us, when shall these things be? and what shall be the sign of thy coming, and of the end of the world?

4 And Jesus answered and said unto them, Take heed that no man deceive you.

5 For many shall come in my name, saying, I am Christ; and shall deceive many.

6 And ye shall hear of wars and rumors of wars: see that ye be not troubled: for all these things must come to pass, but the end is not yet.

7 For nation shall rise against nation, and kingdom against kingdom: and there shall be famines, and pestilences, and earthquakes, in divers places.

8 All these are the beginning of sorrows.

9 Then shall they deliver you up to be afflicted, and shall kill you: and ye shall be hated of all nations for my name's sake.

10 And then shall many be offended, and shall betray one another, and shall hate one another.

11 And many false prophets shall rise, and shall deceive many.

12 And because iniquity shall abound, the love of many shall wax cold.

13 But he that shall endure unto the end, the same shall be saved.

14 And this gospel of the kingdom shall be preached in all the world for a witness unto all nations; and then shall the end come.

Showing that the Restoration was an event of the future—

Rev., fourth chapter:

1 After this I looked, and, behold, a door was opened in heaven: and the first voice which I heard was as it were of a trumpet talking with me; which said, Come up hither, and I will shew thee things which must be hereafter.

Rev., fourteenth chapter:

6 And I saw another angel fly in the midst of heaven, having the everlasting gospel to preach unto them that dwell on the earth, and to every nation, and kindred, and tongue, and people,

7 Saying with a loud voice, Fear God, and give glory to him; for the hour of his judgment is come: and worship him that made heaven, and earth, and the sea, and the fountains of waters.

Showing the nature of an angel—

Rev., twenty-second chapter:

8 And I John saw these things, and heard them. And when I had heard and seen, I fell down to worship before the feet of the angel which shewed me these things.

9 Then saith he unto me, See thou do it not: for I am thy fellow servant, and of thy brethren the prophets, and of them which keep the sayings of this book: worship God.

CHAPTER II.

THE MODE OF OPERATION.

THE foundation and chief advantage of the method of teaching is to set up a negative or opposite to the position taken by the student. This gives him something to talk to or against. Thus some of the advantages accruing from the debate of a question are attained, without the great disadvantage of some person assuming its wrong side, and arguing against truth and conscience.

This is done by stating the views gener_ally held by sectarian (notably Protestant) religionists on any given point in opposition to the views of the Latter-day Saints.

Positions to be sustained by the student:

First. That salvation cannot be attained by belief in Christ and His atonement, without good works.

Second. That the only correct method of baptism is immersion; that it is positively essential to salvation, and is for the remission of sins.

Third. That the Holy Ghost is obtained after belief, repentance and baptism, by the ordi-

Positions generally assumed by sectarians (notably Protestants) to be reasoned away and overthrown by the student:

First. That salvation can be obtained by belief in Christ and His atonement, independent of good works.

Second. That baptism may be administered by sprinkling, pouring or immersion; that it is not positively essential, and not for the remission of sins.

Third. That the Holy Ghost can be obtained by belief in the Lord Jesus Christ, without attend-

nance of laying on of the hands of men having divine authority.

Fourth. That Apostles, Prophets and other inspired teachers and revelation are as necessary to the Church now as ever, and cannot be dispensed with.

Fifth. That the repentant and probably unbaptized thief did not go to heaven direct, but to where Christ went, when He preached to the spirits in prison.

Sixth. That there was a universal apostasy from the true order of the Gospel, and that it has been again restored through the agency of angels and revelation.

Seventh. That no man has a right to preach or administer the Gospel without being divinely authorized by revelation.

ing to any outward ordinances.

Fourth. That Apostles, Prophets and other inspired teachers and revelation were needed in the primitive condition of the Church, but are done away because no longer needed.

Fifth. Had baptism for the remission of sins been essential, the thief on the cross would not have received the promise to be with Christ in Paradise.

Sixth. That the Gospel has been on the earth continuously since the days of the Savior; therefore it was not necessary to restore it in these days.

Seventh. That authority by revelation is not necessary. If a person feels a desire to preach or administer, he is called to do so, especially if he has been educated for the ministry.

The teacher should necessarily be a person of some experience in preaching the Gospel, familiar with the strong arguments, and scriptural proofs sustaining every point.

It is preferable that the class should be composed of young men who express a hearty voluntary desire to identify themselves with it, rather than those who need much persuasion. A strong inclination to learn is a chief essential to progress.

The first meeting of the class should be devoted to talking upon each of the above expressed sectarian views, one after the other, by the teacher, who should explain how to overturn them, or establish the affirmative by reason and scripture.

Then give one of the points to each of the students to speak upon, limiting the time of the pupil to fifteen minutes on a subject.

This should be kept up until each of the pupils has disposed of the whole seven positions. Thus he will be obtaining a knowledge of the principles of the Gospel, becoming informed upon the views of the sectarians regarding them, and acquiring ability to preach at the same time.

The main defect in ordinary theological teaching is that the teacher generally does most of the talking. This should not be the case, as it is not what the pupil hears but what he does and says himself that fastens most firmly upon his mind.

While the students are engaged in the exercises the teacher should be careful to give them all the encouragement possible, at the same time, in a kindly manner, point out errors and defects with a view to their being avoided.

After the seven points have been spoken upon by the class, the teacher should occupy one meeting in explaining how, by the aid of the Spirit of the Lord, each member can deliver a discourse, illustrating this by delivering one himself.

The next thing in order will be for each pupil, by the information he has obtained, to preach a discourse, limited to half an hour, until the whole class has gone through that exercise.

If the young men are fairly or a little over ordinarily intelligent and reasonably educated, the progress attained by this time will be very marked, and in some instances, especially if the teacher has tact and ability, astonishing.

The pupils will be likely to be discouraged on the start, but they should not give up. Faith, patience, perseverance and the aid of the good Spirit will insure success in every instance. Perhaps it would simplify the method by giving the following recapitulation of the foregoing—

First. Study well the scriptural passages.

Second. The teacher should speak on each of the sectarian standpoints, as an opening review.

Third. Each student should be given the points to speak to, until he has spoken on the whole.

Fourth. The teacher should observe the remarks of the pupil, with a view to correction and commendation.

Fifth. The teacher should review the whole, delivering a discourse, as an example.

Sixth. Each of the pupils should alternately do the same.

Seventh. The pupils should be taught that the object is not to learn a discourse by heart, but to acquire knowledge to be brought to their remembrance by the Spirit of God, whenever needed in the discharge of their duties.

The class should be regulated by something like the following—

RULES.

First. For the method to operate successfully and admit of satisfactory progress, there should not be more than twelve pupils in a class.

Second. New pupils should not be admitted later than the second meeting; otherwise progress will be retarded.

Third. Students who absent themselves from two consecutive sessions without a satisfactory excuse should be dropped from the roll.

Fourth. The exercises should invariably be opened and closed with prayer.

Fifth. A secretary should be appointed at the first meeting, whose duty should be to keep and call the roll.

Sixth. The order in which the pupils speak should be according to relative position on the roll.

CHAPTER III.

PLURAL MARRIAGE.

THE chief merit of the method is its directness and practicability. It is not only of use in teaching what are termed the first principles of the Gospel, but can be extended to every truth of the divine plan, by simply setting up an opposite. As the Elders who go abroad are invariably assailed on the subject of polygamy, it may be well for them to be prepared to show that it is sustained by the Bible. Should a class wish to inform themselves on this subject, let them argue against the following common sectarian standpoint—

"Polygamy is not sustained by the Scriptures,"

Using the following and any other suitable passages, and sound reasoning:

SCRIPTURE PASSAGES.

Showing that children born in the polygamous order of marriage were acknowledged and blessed of the Lord—

Gen., sixteenth chapter:

5 And Sarai said unto Abram, My wrong be upon thee: I have given my maid into thy bosom, and when she saw that she had conceived, I was despised in her eyes: the Lord judge between me and thee.

6 But Abram said unto Sarai, Behold thy maid is in thy hand: do to her as it pleaseth thee. And when Sarai dealt hardly with her, she fled from her face.

7 And the angel of the Lord found her by a fountain of water in the wilderness, by the fountain in the way to Shur.

8 And he said, Hagar, Sarai's maid, whence camest thou? and whither wilt thou go? And she said, I flee from the face of my mistress Sarai.

9 And the angel of the Lord said unto her, Return to thy mistress, and submit thyself under her hands.

10 And the angel of the Lord said unto her, I will multiply thy seed exceedingly, that it shall not be numbered for multitude.

11 And the angel of the Lord said unto her, Behold thou art with child, and shall bear a son, and shalt call his name Ishmael; because the Lord hath heard thy affliction.

Gen., twenty-first chapter:

10 Wherefore she said unto Abraham, Cast out this bondwoman and her son: for the son of this bondwoman shall not be heir with my son, even with Isaac.

11 And the thing was very grievous in Abraham's sight because of his son.

12 And God said unto Abraham, Let it not be grievous in thy sight because of the lad, and because of thy bondwoman; in all that Sarah hath said unto thee, hearken ye unto her voice; for in Isaac shall thy seed be called.

13 And also the son of the bondwoman will I make a nation, because he is thy seed.

14 And Abraham rose up early in the morning, and took bread, and a bottle of water, and gave it unto Hagar, putting it on her shoulder, and the child, and sent her away: and she departed, and wandered in the wilderness of Beer-sheba.

15 And the water was spent in the bottle, and she cast the child under one of the shrubs.

16 And she went, and sat her down over against him a good way off, as it were a bowshot: for she said, Let me not see the death of the child. And she sat over against him, and lifted up her voice, and wept.

17 And God heard the voice of the lad; and the angel of God called to Hagar out of heaven, and said unto her, What aileth thee, Hagar? fear not; for God hath heard the voice of the lad where he is.

18 Arise, lift up the lad, and hold him in thine hand; for I will make him a great nation.

19 And God opened her eyes, and she saw a well of water; and she went, and filled the bottle with water, and gave the lad drink.

20 And God was with the lad; and he grew, and dwelt in the wilderness, and became an archer.

Gen., thirty-third chapter:

1 And Jacob lifted up his eyes, and looked, and, behold, Esau came, and with him four hundred men.

And he divided the children unto Leah, and unto Rachel, and unto the two handmaids.

2 And he put the handmaids and their children foremost, and Leah and her children after, and Rachel and Joseph hindermost.

3 And he passed over before them, and bowed himself to the ground seven times, until he came near to his brother.

4 And Esau ran to meet him, and embraced him, and fell on his neck, and kissed him: and they wept.

5 And he lifted up his eyes, and saw the women and the children, and said, Who are those with thee? And he said, The children which God hath graciously given thy servant.

6 Then the handmaidens came near, they and their children, and they bowed themselves.

Gen., twenty-fifth chapter:

1 Then again Abraham took a wife, and her name was Keturah.

2 And she bare him Zimran, and Jokshan, and Medam, and Midian, and Ishbak, and Shuah.

Showing that Abraham's course was approved of God, evidently including his entering·into polygamous marriage relations—

Gen., twenty-sixth chapter:

1 And there was a famine in the land, besides the first famine that was in the days of Abraham. And Isaac went unto Abimelech king of the Philistines unto Gerar.

2 And the Lord appeared unto him, and said, Go

not down into Egypt; dwell in the land which I shall tell thee of.

3 Sojourn in this land, and I will be with thee, and will bless thee: for unto thee, and unto thy seed, I will give all these countries, and I will perform the oath which I sware unto Abraham thy father;

4 And I will make thy seed to multiply as the stars of heaven, and will give unto thy seed all these countries; and in thy seed shall all the nations of the earth be blessed.

5 Because that Abraham obeyed my voice, and kept my charge, my commandments, my statutes, and my laws.

Showing that Moses was a polygamist, and that the Lord was sorely displeased with his being interfered with in that relation—

Exodus, second chapter:

16 Now the priest of Midian had seven daughters; and they came and drew water, and filled the troughs to water their father's flock.

17 And the shepherds came and drove them away: but Moses stood up and helped them, and watered their flock.

18 And when they came to Reuel their father, he said, How is it that ye are come so soon to-day?

19 And they said, An Egyptian delivered us out of the hand of the shepherds, and also drew water enough for us, and watered the flock.

20 And he said unto his daughters, And where

is he? why is it that ye have left the man? call him, that he may eat bread.

21 And Moses was content to dwell with the man: and he gave Moses Zipporah his daughter.

Numbers, twelfth chapter:

1 And Miriam and Aaron spake against Moses because of the Ethiopian woman whom he had married: for he had married an Ethiopian woman.

2 And they said, Hath the Lord indeed spoken only by Moses? hath he not spoken also by us? And the Lord heard it.

3 (Now the man Moses was very meek, above all the men which were upon the face of the earth.)

4 And the Lord spake suddenly unto Moses, and unto Aaron, and unto Miriam, Come out ye three unto the tabernacle of the congregation. And they three came out.

5 And the Lord came down in the pillar of the cloud, and stood in the door of the tabernacle, and called Aaron and Miriam: and they both came forth.

6 And he said, Hear now my words: If there be a prophet among you, I the Lord will make myself known unto him in a vision, and will speak unto him in a dream.

7 My servant Moses is not so, who is faithful in all mine house.

8 With him will I speak mouth to mouth, even apparently, and not in dark speeches; and the similitude of the Lord shall he behold; wherefore then were ye not afraid to speak against my servant Moses?

9 And the anger of the Lord was kindled against them; and he departed.

10 And the cloud departed from off the tabernacle; and, behold, Miriam became leprous, white as snow: and Aaron looked upon Miriam, and, behold, she was leprous.

11 And Aaron said unto Moses, Alas, my lord, I beseech thee, lay not the sin upon us, wherein we have done foolishly, and wherein we have sinned.

12 Let her not be as one dead, of whom the flesh is half consumed when he cometh out of his mother's womb.

13 And Moses cried unto the Lord, saying, Heal her now, O God, I beseech thee.

The following passage is sometimes used against polygamy, but it would be as sensible to use it to prove that a man should have but one horse—

Deut., seventeenth chapter:

14 When thou art come unto the land which the Lord thy God giveth thee, and shalt possess it, and shalt dwell therein, and shalt say, I will set a king over me, like as all the nations that are about me;

15 Thou shalt in any wise set him king over thee, whom the Lord thy God shall choose: one from among thy brethren shalt thou set king over thee: thou mayest not set a stranger over thee, which is not thy brother.

16 But he shall not multiply horses to himself, nor cause the people to return to Egypt, to the end that he should multiply horses: forasmuch as the

Lord hath said unto you, Ye shall henceforth return no more that way.

17 Neither shall he multiply wives to himself, that
his heart turn not away; neither shall he greatly multiply to himself silver and gold.

This shows a plain recognition, by the law
of the Lord, of polygamy, by providing for
possible conditions that might arise under it—

Deut., twenty-first chapter:

15 If a man have two wives, one beloved, and
another hated, and they have borne him children,
both the beloved and the hated; and if the firstborn
son be hers that was hated:

16 Then it shall be, when he maketh his sons to
inherit that which he hath, that he may not make the
son of the beloved firstborn before the son of the
hated, which is indeed the firstborn:

17 But he shall acknowledge the son of the hated
for the firstborn, by giving him a double portion of
all that he hath: for he is the beginning of his
strength; the right of the firstborn is his.

This clause of the law rendered polygamy, under some circumstances, compulsory, there being no provision for the ex-
emption from its requirements of a man
already married—

Deut., twenty-fifth chapter:

5 If brethren dwell together, and one of them

die, and have no child, the wife of the dead shall not marry without unto a stranger: her husband's brother shall go in unto her, and take her to him to wife, and perform the duty of a husband's brother unto her.

6 And it shall be, that the firstborn which she beareth shall succeed in the name of his brother which is dead, that his name be not put out of Israel.

Showing how God heard and honored the prayer of a polygamous wife—

1 Samuel, first chapter:

1 Now there was a certain man of Ramathaim-zophim, of mount Ephraim, and his name was Elkanah, the son of Jeroham, the son of Elihu, the son of Tohu, the son of Zuph, an Ephrathite.

2 And he had two wives; the name of the one was Hannah, and the name of the other Peninnah: and Peninnah had children, but Hannah had no children.

11 And she vowed a vow, and said, O Lord of hosts, if thou wilt indeed look on the affliction of thine handmaid, and remember me, and not forget thine handmaid, but wilt give unto thy handmaid a man child, then I will give him unto the Lord all the days of his life, and there shall no razor come upon his head.

20 Wherefore it came to pass, when the time was come about after Hannah had conceived, that she bare a son, and called his name Samuel, saying, Because I have asked him of the Lord.

David, a polygamist, in favor and communion with God—

1 Samuel, thirtieth chapter:

5 And David's two wives were taken captives, Ahinoam the Jezreelitess, and Abigail the wife of Nabal the Carmelite.

6 And David was greatly distressed; for the people spake of stoning him, because the soul of all the people was grieved, every man for his sons and for his daughters: but David encouraged himself in the Lord his God.

7 And David said to Abiathar the priest, Ahimelech's son, I pray thee, bring me hither the ephod. And Abiathar brought thither the ephod to David.

8 And David inquired at the Lord, saying, Shall I pursue after this troop? shall I overtake them? And he answered him, Pursue: for thou shalt surely overtake them, and without fail recover all.

Showing in what manner David and Solomon sinned, etc.—

2 Samuel, twelfth chapter:

7 And Nathan said to David, Thou art the man. Thus saith the Lord God of Israel, I anointed thee king over Israel, and I delivered thee out of the hand of Saul;

8 And I gave thee thy master's house, and thy master's wives into thy bosom, and gave thee the house of Israel and of Judah; and if that had been too little, I would moreover have given unto thee such and such things.

9 Wherefore hast thou despised the commandment of the Lord, to do evil in his sight? thou hast killed Uriah the Hittite with the sword, and hast

taken his wife to be thy wife, and hast slain him with the sword of the children of Ammon.

10 Now therefore the sword shall never depart from thine house; because thou hast despised me and hast taken the wife of Uriah the Hittite to be thy wife.

1 Kings, eleventh chapter:

1 But king Solomon loved many strange women, together with the daughter of Pharaoh, women of the Moabites, Ammonites, Edomites, Zidonians, and Hittites;

2 Of the nations concerning which the Lord said unto the children of Israel, Ye shall not go in to them, neither shall they come in unto you: for surely they will turn away your heart after their gods; Solomon clave unto these in love.

3 And he had seven hundred wives, princesses, and three hundred concubines: and his wives turned away his heart.

1 Kings, fifteenth chapter:

5 Because David did that which was right in the eyes of the Lord, and turned not aside from any thing that he commanded him all the days of his life, save only in the matter of Uriah the Hittite.

2 Chron., thirteenth chapter:

16 And the children of Israel fled before Judah: and God delivered them into their hand.

17 And Abijah and his people slew them with a great slaughter: so there fell down slain of Israel five hundred thousand chosen men.

18 Thus the children of Israel were brought un-

der at that time, and the children of Judah pre-
vailed, because they relied upon the Lord God of
their fathers.

19 And Abijah pursued after Jeroboam, and took
cities from him, Beth-el with the towns thereof, and
Jeshanah with the towns thereof, and Ephraim with
the towns thereof.

20 Neither did Jeroboam recover strength again in
the days of Abijah: and the Lord struck him, and he
died.

21 But Abijah waxed mighty, and married four-
teen wives, and begat twenty and two sons, and
sixteen daughters.

2 Chron., twenty-fourth chapter:

1 Joash was seven years old when he began to
reign, and he reigned forty years in Jerusalem. His
mother's name also was Zibiah of Beersheba.

2 And Joash did that which was right in the sight
of the Lord all the days of Jehoiada the priest.

4 And Jehoiada took for him two wives; and he
begat sons and daughters.

Something yet to be fulfilled—

Isaiah, fourth chapter:

1 And in that day seven women shall take hold
of one man, saying, We will eat our own bread, and
wear our own apparel; only let us be called by thy
name, to take away our reproach.

Some people confound polygamy with
adultery, yet the Bible shows the former

was honored and blessed while the latter was punished with death—

Deut., twenty-second chapter:

22 If a man be found lying with a woman married to a husband, they shall both of them die, both the man that lay with the woman, and the woman: so shalt thou put away evil from Israel.

23 If a damsel that is a virgin be betrothed unto a husband, and a man find her in the city, and lie with her;

24 Then ye shall bring them both out unto the gate of that city, and ye shall stone them with stones that they die; the damsel, because she cried not, being in the city; and the man, because he hath humbled his neighbor's wife: so thou shalt put away evil from among you.

Deut., twenty-third chapter:

2 A bastard shall not enter into the congregation of the Lord: even to his tenth generation shall he not enter into the congregation of the Lord.

The Savior recognized the law of God as set forth in the Bible—

Matt., fifth chapter:

17 Think not that I am come to destroy the law, or the prophets: I am not come to destroy, but to fulfil.

18 For verily I say unto you, Till heaven and earth pass, one jot or one tittle shall in no wise pass from the law till all be fulfilled.

Jesus denounces a species of polygamy largely existing in the world—the putting away of one wife in order to take another—

Matt., nineteenth chapter:
9 And I say unto you, Whosoever shall put away his wife, except it be for fornication, and shall marry another, committeth adultery: and whoso marrieth her which is put away doth commit adultery.

Mark, tenth chapter:
11 And he saith unto them, Whosoever shall put away his wife, and marry another, committeth adultery against her.

Showing that every woman is entitled to a husband—

I Cor., second chapter:
11 Nevertheless neither is the man without the woman, neither the woman without the man, in the Lord.

The following passages are sometimes used in opposition to polygamy, but even if it be granted that these officers should have *but* one wife, this would imply the existence of polygamy at that time, and that others were not placed under that restriction. It shows, however, they were required to be married men, and the inser-

4

tion of *at least* is equally as admissible as *but*—

1 Tim., third chapter:

1 This is a true saying, If a man desire the office of a bishop, he desireth a good work.

2 A bishop then must be blameless, the husband of one wife, vigilant, sober, of good behavior, given to hospitality, apt to teach;

12 Let the deacons be the husbands of one wife, ruling their children and their own houses well.

The progeny of a polygamist are to be honored—

Rev., twenty-first chapter:

12 And had a wall great and high, and had twelve gates, and at the gates twelve angels, and names written thereon, which are the names of the twelve tribes of the children of Israel.

The following is fulfilled in the compulsory celibacy of the Catholic clergy and not improbably in the attempted suppression of polygamy—

1 Tim., fourth chapter:

1 Now the Spirit speaketh expressly, that in the latter times some shall depart from the faith, giving heed to seducing spirits, and doctrines of devils;

2 Speaking lies in hypocrisy: having their conscience seared with a hot iron;

3 *Forbidding to marry*, and commanding to ab-

stain from meats, which God hath created to be received with thanksgiving of them which believe and know the truth.

As to what some of Abraham's works were, the record shows—

John, eighth chapter:

39 They answered and said unto him, Abraham is our father. Jesus saith unto them, If ye were Abraham's children, ye would do the works of Abraham.

The working of this simple method of teaching need not be confined to matters pertaining to the Bible, but could be extended to all the revelations, especially those of the Book of Doctrine and Covenants and Book of Mormon, with which our young people should, so far as practicable, be made familiar.

CHAPTER IV.

HINTS ON PREACHING.

The effect of preaching, especially that of inexperienced Elders, is frequently marred by defects of delivery which could, in most instances, be obviated by thought and attention. It is always easier to get rid of a defect in the earlier stages of experience, than when it becomes more or less a confirmed habit.

I submit the following hints, in the hope that they may prove of some benefit:

1. Do not shut your eyes, nor look at the ceiling. In other words, do not look away from, but squarely at your audience. Consider your congregation an individualism that you wish to bring to your way of thinking.

2. If you are predisposed to be aggressive, cultivate a persuasive manner. The former style often brings needless opposition, and while it may convince the intellect of the listener, seldom, if ever, wins the heart.

3. Without paying too much attention to gesture and elocution, it is well to suit the action to the word and the word to the action, and throw special force into those phrases containing the leading points you wish to convey.

4. Never imitate the style and manner of another speaker, however excel-

lent may be the model. Be natural and ad-
here to your own style, because it is natural.
No other is adapted to you, any more than
another man's nose would be adapted to
your style of face.

5. Pay attention to accentuation. Pro-
nounce every word clearly and distinctly
before beginning to utter another. Each
word should be a well defined entity, not
merged into another. What might be
termed the confluent type of public speaking—the words running into one another in
a sort of mass—is one to be strictly avoided.

6. In beginning to address an audience, assume an easy attitude and avoid
hurry, which leads to confusion and failure.
Rapid utterance is a common fault of young
speakers, as with young swimmers—a few
quick, excited strokes, and down they go.

7. The first consideration in the suc-
cessful preaching of the Gospel is to obtain, by a godly life and through prayer and
faith, the Spirit of the Lord, without which
no man will possess power for good.

8. It is of great importance to have
the mind stored with the principles of
truth, that you may have something to say.

Those who imagine the Spirit will do everything for them will be disappointed. The chief office of the Spirit is to aid the Elder in his search for knowledge, bring what he has learned to his memory, when occasion requires, and give him freedom and facility of utterance. The Lord does not place a premium upon indolence. You cannot draw water out of a dry well. Neither will intelligence and truth be brought forth from an empty mind. Study and reflect; fill your mind with knowledge. The Spirit will do the rest.

9. Be in earnest. Feel the importance of the message you bear. Show your earnestness in the vigor of your speech. Do not mumble and mutter, but speak right out, always sufficiently loud for all your audience to hear you distinctiy. You will never convince others of the correctness of any matter regarding which you appear, by your manner or otherwise, to be in some doubt yourself.

10. Never speak upon subjects you do not clearly understand. You can never make plain to others what is not clear to yourself. Let mysteries alone.

11. Do not endeavor to be a florid speaker. Your chief aim should be clearness and simplicity, the object being to convey to others your own sincere convictions. Use the simplest words that will correctly define your meaning. There may be persons in your congregation who would not understand the more unusual words; therefore, when simple language is used, it will always be comprehended by the greatest possible number. Besides, there is beauty in simplicity.

12. Many men with good natural abilities for public speaking fail from being unable to control their feelings while before an audience. School yourself to be collected, and never let your language get ahead of your ideas. In other words, do not force your ideas to conform to your language; your language must conform to your ideas. Always speak to an idea, thought or truth as it may be brought to your mind by the Spirit. Give the Spirit time to suggest, and utter the thoughts as they present themselves. Do not be in haste to sit down until you are certain the Spirit will not come to your aid.

13. Do not speak for the purpose of gaining the applause of men. If you do you will not obtain much aid from the Spirit of the Lord. Let your aim be to please God, and take your chance as to your efforts pleasing men; at the same time always avoid being unnecessarily offensive to your fellow creatures.

14. When you succeed in preaching with freedom, by the aid of the Spirit of Truth, do not afterwards feed your vanity in fishing for compliments by asking people how they liked your discourse. Cultivate a spirit of humility and give God the glory. If you do not you will meet with disappointment, for not only the Lord, but clear-sighted men and women will observe your weakness.

15. Avoid the too common habit of finishing and beginning several times over during your discourse. No one who does this can retain the full sympathy and patience of an audience. When a congregation has obtained an impression that a speaker is about to wind up his remarks, and he starts off anew, the effect is generally unfavorable.

Besides the hints given above, I may state my belief that many men of good ability, and who in many respects enjoy the spirit of their callings, fail in clearly expressing their views publicly from a deficiency in what might be termed the constructive faculty. I am satisfied that this can, however, be cultivated by a little attention and the aid of the Good Spirit.

A man may have a large amount of building materials accumulated, but if they be merely thrown together in a sort of jumbled mass, without the application of the principles of construction, they will be an unsightly heap, entirely devoid of beauty, because without proper form. A skilful use of the laws of architecture and building would, however, from the same substances, produce a handsome structure.

So it is with a man whose mind is stored with the principles of truth. He may be unable to present, in acceptable shape, the intelligence of which he is possessed. On the other hand, one whose store of information is of no greater extent may be able, especially if endowed with the Spirit of the Gospel, to captivate and convince his auditors.

Many men possess the ability to preach the Gospel clearly and powerfully, and are not aware of it, because they have not struck that element of success, and have been floundering in consequence.

A case in point comes to my mind. A young man of good ability, while on a mission a few years ago, got the idea that he could not preach, because he had made several failures. One evening, after having spoken in a public meeting and occupied the time in desperately catching at ideas "on the wing," grasping and groping after them like a drowning man clutching at straws, he was downcast, and informed a friend that he felt as if he would give preaching up for a bad job. His friend reasoned to show him that he certainly could, by the blessing of God, preach the Gospel, especially as that was a portion of his calling. He asked him if he knew Joseph Smith to be a Prophet? Of course he answered yes.

He next inquired if he had any reasons and evidences to offer for making that claim. After reflecting a few moments, he said he had a good many.

He then asked him successively a num-

ber of other questions, and whether he
could adduce reasons to sustain the points,
he giving to each an affirmative answer,
such as—

"Do you understand that the sects called
Christendom are a departure from the true
order of the Gospel?"

"Do you know what the ordinances of
the Gospel are, and for what administered?"

"Do you know the organization of the
true Church?"

"Do you understand that the Gospel has
been restored in power, purity and com-
pleteness in this age?"

These and hundreds of other positions
can be sustained by any well informed
Elder, and he was advised, next time he ad-
dressed a congregation, to take up the point
first suggested to his mind by the Spirit
with the scriptural evidence and sound ar-
gument at his command, and when that
was disposed of to take up the next point
presented, and so on until the Spirit said
stop.

Next time the Elder spoke he delivered
a clear, pointed and convincing discourse
on the first principles of the Gospel, the

apostate condition of Christendom, and the restoration of the true plan of salvation.

This was not because he delivered a prepared sermon, for he did not do so, but by giving definite shape to the information that was in him, he was enabled to present a clear enunciation of his views.

The manner of seizing upon a main point and properly disposing of it, is in harmony with this way of teaching the principles of the Gospel, by having something to speak to, giving order, shape, construction and consequent force and beauty to the discourse.

www.ingramcontent.com/pod-product-compliance
Lightning Source LLC
Chambersburg PA
CBHW031749090426
42739CB00008B/935